The Voice from the Cross

Donald Coggan was Archbishop of Canterbury from 1974 to 1980. He is the author of many books, on subjects ranging from theology and biblical studies to biography and spirituality; his most recent title was *God of Hope* (HarperCollins 1991). He now lives in Winchester with his wife Jean, to whom he has been married for fifty-seven years. They have two daughters.

The Voice from the Cross

THE SEVEN WORDS
OF JESUS

Donald Coggan

TRI∧NGLE

First published 1993
Triangle
SPCK
Holy Trinity Church
Marylebone Road
London NW1 4DU

British Library Cataloguing in Publication Data
A catalogue record for this book is available from the British Library.
ISBN 0-281-04655-7

Typeset by Inforum, Rowlands Castle, Hants
Printed and bound in Great Britain by
BPCC Hazells Ltd
Member of BPCC Ltd

For Jean

Contents

Contents

Foreword

*I*t may be – I would like to think it – that this little book will be of help to some who have the privilege of conducting the Three Hours Service on Good Friday. But it is by no means only such people whom I have had in mind in putting these chapters together. I have envisaged a far wider readership.

I have been thinking of those many Christians – and perhaps some who would not claim that title – who feel strangely drawn to the man on the cross, lifted up to die. There is a mystery about the cross. It has a magnetic power. It has a way of speaking to a tortured world, a twisted conscience, a torn heart. It has a way of sorting us out.

We shall never plumb the full meaning of the seven words which the Evangelists record as having been spoken by our Lord as he hung on the cross. But to listen to them once again, so old, so new, is an exercise which carries with it a reward of its own. 'When I am lifted up from the earth I shall draw everyone to myself' (John 12.32).

Hence this book. Good listening!

Winchester
July 1992

Donald Coggan

1

The Miracle of Forgiveness

There were two others with him, criminals who were being led out to execution; and when they reached the place called The Skull they crucified him there, and the criminals with him, one on his right and the other on his left. Jesus said, 'Father, forgive them; they do not know what they are doing.'

They shared out his clothes by casting lots. The people stood looking on, and their rulers jeered at him: 'He saved others: now let him save himself, if this is God's Messiah, his Chosen.' The soldiers joined in the mockery and came forward offering him sour wine. 'If you are the king of the Jews,' they said, 'save yourself.' There was an inscription above his head which ran: 'This is the king of the Jews.'

Luke 23.32–8

> Two trees
>   proclaim in spring
>   a word to a world.
> One exploding
>   into blossom
>   trumpets glory.
> One stretching
>   dead limbs
>   holds the empty
>   body of God.
> Both speak
>   with due reserve
>   into the listening
>   ear of the world.

Ralph Wright

'Father, forgive them; they do not know what they are doing.'

Luke 23.34

Didn't they know – those men who drove the nails into the hands and feet of the crucified? No. They had never had the opportunity of sitting at the feet of the young rabbi from Galilee. So far as he was concerned, they had been brought up in the dark. Now, coarsened by the work that they were compelled to do, they were getting on with a cruel and callous job. Nor did the criminals know, one on each side of the crucified, poor wretched ruffians that they were. Behind the soldiers and the ruffians was a system for which they could not be blamed; a *state* which could breed a Herod, a Pontius Pilate; a *Church* which could breed a Caiaphas. What kind of system was this that could think up crucifixion as a method of dealing with crime, as if cruelty could wipe out rebellion!

No doubt the soldiers and malefactors had sinned and sinned grievously. They were in some measure responsible for the positions in which they found themselves. But in very large measure they were victims of the national set-up of which they were, willy-nilly, a part. They didn't know what they were doing. Perhaps something of the enormity of the crucifixion of the man on the middle cross dawned as they watched him suffer? Never man suffered like this man.

There are two kinds of ignorance: the ignorance which is culpable and the ignorance which is not. The two sometimes merge, but the difference is reasonably clear. As God today looks down on the world he made and for which his Son was content to die, he sees a situation comparable to that of the first Good Friday. Millions in our world cannot be blamed for their ignorance of God – they have never heard the name which is above every name. In our own country, and in the West generally, millions of young people are brought up in almost total ignorance of the elements of the Christian faith; the very name of Jesus is only heard as an expletive. Who is to blame – these youngsters or their parents? These youngsters or a system which seems to deny the very essence of what Christianity stands for; which cries out that it matters not what you believe, that freedom means licence, that having and getting are more important than being? Who is to blame, if this is in the very air that they breathe?

And yet . . . it is easy to lay all the blame at the door of the state or even of the Church. There is that in us which prefers darkness to light because our deeds are evil (John 3.19). There are churches whose very presence reminds us of eternal realities. There are Bibles available. There are sources of knowledge and inspiration awaiting our asking. 'How often have I longed to gather your children, as a hen gathers her brood under her wings; *but you would not let me*' (Luke 13.34). There is ignorance for which we cannot be blamed; there is ignorance for which we must be blamed. But both kinds are terrible because they lie behind the crucifixion of the Son of God.

'Father, forgive them . . .' So says the first word
from the cross.

After Coventry Cathedral had been blitzed by the Germans in 1940, the authorities raised up in the ruins a
huge cross made of two charred beams of wood. On the
cross they inscribed the words 'Father, forgive'. Two
words, mark you; not three. The omission of the word
'them' is eloquent. They might have said 'Forgive the
Germans who perpetrated this awful deed; forgive *them*.'
What that omission says by its very silence is this: We are
all in on the tragedy of war. The hands of all of us are
stained. We all share in what John calls 'the sin of the
world' (John 1.29), its hate, its lust for power, its envy.
Guilt is racial as well as personal, and we all share its
taint. Father, forgive the great powers who spend billions
on the production of arms while billions of human
beings starve . . . Father, forgive.

The theme of this first word is forgiveness. That had
been a major theme of Jesus during his teaching ministry. Again and again he had insisted on our primary need
of forgiveness, God's forgiveness and that of our fellows.
He had incorporated this in the prayer which he taught
his disciples: 'Forgive us the wrong we have done, as we
have forgiven those who wronged us'. He had elabo-
rated it in a couple of sentences of alarming clarity: 'For
if you forgive the wrongs they have done, your heavenly
Father will also forgive you; but if you do not forgive
others, then your Father will not forgive the wrongs that
you have done' (Matthew 6.12–15). This sounds tough.

Is it a threat? Not at all. Just a statement of fact. If I insist in remaining unforgiving to someone who has injured me, I shall, of course, injure that person. But it is even more certain that I shall injure *myself*. I become hardened. A kind of callus grows over my heart, which thwarts my powers of receptivity until I find myself unable to open up to the forgiveness of God. 'The measure you give is the measure you will receive' (Mark 4.24). The grain of the universe goes that way; you will only damage yourself if you try to pit yourself against it.

Forgiveness is one of the most therapeutic forces in the world. Forgive, and you will receive the forgiveness of God, and the after-effects of that forgiveness will astound you. Right relationships with God and with our fellows result in an inner serenity, a peace of heart and mind which often have physical and nervous benefits of surprising power. Many of our hospital beds would be empty if their occupants had learnt this basic lesson.

Illustrations of this truth in modern life abound. I recall a visit to Northern Ireland where, in Belfast, Londonderry and Armagh, I saw evidence of hate in blitzed pubs, damaged homes and wounded bodies and minds. But in the midst of it all I saw signs of hope, and these were always connected with forgiveness. In the Falls Road area of Belfast I met a man whose son had been shot dead. Yet in that father was no trace of bitterness, no element of unforgivingness. As he spoke to me that morning, he ministered to me. Not many miles away, in the seaside beauty of Corrymeela, I saw a community of Roman Catholics and Protestants whose sole purpose was to sow love where there is hate and to bind up the wounds created by war. Forgiveness was breaking through as the sun's rays break through the fog. That community ministered to me.

In Israel, not many miles outside Jerusalem, is another community, *Neve Shalom*, where men and women of goodwill take little Israeli children and an equal number of Arab children, teach them to live together, play together, learn one another's languages, in the hope that they will, as they grow older, inject love where there is hate, forgiveness where there is resentment. A frail experiment? Maybe. But light 'shines in the darkness, and the darkness has never mastered it' (John 1.5).

In South Africa I met Nelson Mandela. Have you noticed the lack of bitterness, the absence of vengeance in his utterances, after twenty-seven years in prison? Forgiveness, I repeat, is therapeutic.

'Father, forgive them . . .' When I listen to this word from the cross, I find myself face to face with a miracle, the miracle of a holy God forgiving me, an unholy sinner. When I receive that forgiveness and open up my being to its warmth, a process begins in me by which I am able to forgive others. 'You must forgive as the Lord forgave you' (Colossians 3.13). When I begin to realise the immensity of the divine compassion, I cannot long withhold forgiveness from others.

O Lord Jesus Christ,
   touch me with those hands of thine
   which the sins of men and sins of mine pierced
      with the nails;
   and forgive mine ignorances, many and oft;
   for, Lord I knew not, indeed I know not
      what I did in my sinning against thee.
Touch me to forgive
   and to bless, O Lord,
      for thine endless mercies' sake.

Eric Milner-White

Give us, O Lord, the spirit of humility, that we may
never presume upon thy mercy, but live as those who
have been much forgiven.

Make us tender and compassionate towards others;
and grant that we may show forth in our lives that
enduring love which alone can triumph over all the
powers of evil; after the example of thy Son Jesus Christ
our Lord.

George Timms (after C. J. Vaughan)

Sinless Lord, you prayed for the forgiveness of those who drove nails into your hands and feet:

help us sinners to grasp the immensity of your love and the triviality of the wrongs inflicted on us, and to forgive as you did.

For your sake.

Michael Botting

2

Light on Death

One of the criminals hanging there taunted him: 'Are you not the Messiah? Save yourself, and us.' But the other rebuked him: 'Have you no fear of God? You are under the same sentence as he is. In our case it is plain justice; we are paying the price for our misdeeds. But this man has done nothing wrong.' And he said, 'Jesus, remember me when you come to your throne.' Jesus answered, 'Truly I tell you: today you will be with me in Paradise.'

Luke 23.39–43

The other gods were strong,
but thou wast weak;
they rode, but thou
didst stagger to a throne.
But to our wounds
only God's wounds can speak,
And not a god has wounds
but thou alone.

Edward Shillito

'Truly I tell you: today you will be with me in Paradise.'

Luke 23.43

Who was this man to whom the second word from the cross was addressed? We know next to nothing about him. Perhaps he was a highwayman (there were plenty of them on the roads), a brigand, a thug. Why was he there that day? Was it the lure of quick money? Bad company? The fear of being thought a 'softie' if he didn't join the gang? We do not know precisely. Anyway, justice had caught up with him and there he was, strung up to die, with not much time to go before the end.

His tired eyes strayed towards the man on the cross next to him. He was young, in his early thirties, perhaps, though it was difficult to judge a man's age when he was being crucified. But there was something unusual about him, hard to define – a kind of radiance, something almost 'kingly', though it seemed absurd to think in terms of kingliness when the figure was naked and torn and bleeding. 'King of the Jews', they had said of him. Perhaps there was some truth in their mockery. Perhaps he had a kingdom – death surely could not be the end for a man like that? Could he, a common thug, who had messed up his life, somehow be linked with *him*?

Then it happened. The man on the middle cross, forgetful of his own distress, spoke with him, answered his plea of 'Jesus, remember me when you come to your throne'; answered directly, positively, promptly: 'Truly, I tell you: today you will be with me in Paradise.'

We will come back to that in a moment. But first, two minor points may be touched on for further thought when we have leisure later:

The punctuation. It is possible that the word 'today' should go with the introductory words 'truly I tell you', thus adding a measure of emphasis to the words which precede it. But it is more likely that it should be taken, as it is in most translations, with the words which follow it – 'today you will be with me in Paradise.' If so, the saying points to the immediacy of forgiveness and new-ness of life – cross the river and there is a welcome! Paul, later on, was to put it in memorable words: 'to depart and be with Christ' (Philippians 1.23).

'In Paradise'. The word is Persian and means a garden, a park, an enclosure. People have striven hard to find pictures which convey the idea of a blissful after-life. The writer of Revelation depicted the new heaven as a city of pure gold, bright as clear glass, its foundations adorned with precious stones of every kind (Revelation 21.18–21). That imagery will, no doubt, help some, but I for one find the horticultural more helpful than the architectural. A park or garden speaks of serenity and beauty. And it speaks of ongoing activity, of gardeners in co-operation with the creator – there is little beauty in a park where no work is done! Heaven thought of in these terms speaks of growth, development, creativity, of creatures and creator in happy collusion.

Now to the main thrust of this word from the cross – you, me, Paradise. What has this to say about death and that other world towards which we all inexorably move? Let me quote you two sentences from the writings of J. Neville Figgis, Anglican historian and theologian, sentences with which, on first sight, you may violently disagree. Here they are: 'Religion is fundamentally concerned with the other world. Ultimately, the criterion of any religion lies in what it has to tell us of Death.' Surely, we do not believe that? All our activist tendencies cry out in protest. It is *this* life that matters, we assert; how we live, what we do, in the here and now. Religion is not 'pie in the sky when we die'. If it were, the Marxists would be right in calling it the opiate of the people. Get on with living *now*. Let the after-life look after itself.

There is something to be said for our protest. We could quote William Temple's saying that the Christian faith is the most materialistic of all the religions. He was right, for Christianity springs from the incarnation of Jesus, the Word made flesh. It is securely earthed. Its roots go down deep into the soil of life as it now is, in all its glory and its misery.

There is, however, another side to the matter, and we neglect it at our peril. Authentic Christianity always keeps the end in view. It has to do with human destiny, with our dying and with what lies on the far side of death. J. S. Whale, in a series of lectures delivered to packed audiences in Cambridge during the Second World War, put it this way:

Dying is inevitable, but arriving at the destination God offers to me is not inevitable. It is not impossible to go out of the way and fail to arrive . . . The curious modern heresy that everything is bound to come right in the end is so frivolous that I will not insult you by refuting it. 'I remember', said Dr Johnson on one occasion, 'that my Maker has said that he will place the sheep on his right hand and the goats on the left.' That is a solemn truth which only the empty-headed and empty-hearted will neglect. It strikes at the very root of life and destiny.

The then Master of Emmanuel College, Cambridge, Professor Derek Brewer, writing in 1984, protested against

> the now generally accepted view that there is no human life other than our ordinary life of sense-experience bound to matter and time. Most of the clergy seem to accept this view as completely as the vast post-Christian majority. The notion of Heaven as a valid objective for personal striving is never presented in sermons, and the notion of Hell is dismissed as barbarous. Personal survival is neither preached nor, except by a few bold and traditional spirits, believed.

Exaggerated? Perhaps. But who is to say that the rebuke is undeserved or the warning not to be heeded? And who can deny that the teaching of Jesus, as it has come down to us in the Gospels, points very clearly to a judgement day when an account must be rendered, to a reward to be attained and a hell to be shunned? Human beings are *in via*, on the road.

At the heart of this word from the cross are the two monosyllables – 'with me'. For Christians, that is the very core, the essence, of all they hold dearest about the after-life. When a person, baptised into Christ's body, confirmed in his faith, sent on his mission, filled with his grace, spends his or her life in the divine companionship, the most awful reality he or she can contemplate is separation from him. What would it be to be cut off from *that*? In a word, it would be hell.

The reverse of all that is heaven. It is of this that the man on the middle cross speaks in this grand affirmation – 'today . . . with me . . .'

It is an astonishing statement. What had that ruffian to offer? Nothing but the dregs of a life ill-lived and now fading out in disaster, and the glimmer of a hope and trust in the efficacy of the man next to him. What did he understand about Jesus? Very little. But enough to know that he could cast his hopes on him and not be disappointed. That was all that was asked of him. 'Anyone who comes to me I will never turn away' (John 6.37), not even when he comes *in extremis*. Such is the divine compassion.

'With me' – Paul was to put the Christian approach to death in a trenchant sentence: 'We are confident, I say, and would rather be exiled from the body and *make our home with the Lord*' (2 Corinthians 5.8). With him – and *like* him? John would dare to affirm even that. In his first Letter he is quite prepared to be agnostic in large degree about the after-life – he had better be; aren't we all? 'What we shall be has not yet been disclosed.' Death is surrounded with mystery; it is no good pretending that it is not. 'But', he goes on, and the agnosticism turns to the certainty of faith, 'we know that when Christ appears *we shall be like him*, because we shall see him as he is' (1 John 3.2).

If that – to be 'like him' – be our burning passion in this life, that passion will be consummated in the next. No wonder that John comments 'Everyone who has grasped this hope makes himself pure'; Christian hope has a strong ethical streak to it.

'With me' – 'like him'. A light shines beyond the mystery of death – 'With Christ, which is far better.' Thanks be to God.

O Christ, the King of glory,
     when you had vanquished the sting of death
you opened the kingdom of heaven
     to all who believe in you.
Accept our praise for your surpassing love
     in dying for us sinners.
Open your kingdom to us
     as you did to the penitent thief;
and remember us now, O Lord,
     and in the hour of our death,
for your great mercy's sake.

Frank Colquhoun

Lord Jesus Christ, the friend of sinners, who taught us of
a Father's love that rejoiced in the return of a prodigal
son, and even in the hour of death gave to a penitent
thief the promise of thy continued presence:

We thank thee for this word of reassurance that death
cannot separate us from thy love, and pray that as we
grow in understanding of thy cross, we may draw nearer
to our Father's home.

Basil Naylor

O Lord Jesus Christ,
　　look upon me with those eyes of thine
　　wherewith thou didst look upon the robber
　　　　on the road:
That with him I may confess my sin and beseech
　　　　thee humbly,
　　'Lord remember me when thou comest in
　　　　thy kingdom';
　　and by the same voice be comforted;
　　　　for thine endless mercies' sake.

Eric Milner-White

3
The Therapy of Caring

When the soldiers had crucified Jesus they took his clothes and, leaving aside the tunic, divided them into four parts, one for each soldier. The tunic was seamless, woven in one piece throughout; so they said to one another, 'We must not tear this; let us toss for it.' Thus the text of scripture came true; 'They shared my garments among them, and cast lots for my clothing.'

That is what the soldiers did. Meanwhile near the cross on which Jesus hung, his mother was standing with her sister, Mary wife of Clopas, and Mary of Magdala. Seeing his mother, and the disciple whom he loved standing beside her, Jesus said to her, 'Mother, there is your son'; and to the disciple, 'There is your mother'; and from that moment the disciple took her into his home.

John 19.23–7

> Drained is love in making full;
>   Bound in setting others free;
> Poor in making many rich;
>   Weak in giving power to be.
>
> Therefore he who thee reveals
>   Hangs, O Father, on that Tree
> Helpless, and the nails and thorns
>   Tell of what thy love must be.
>
> Thou art God; no monarch thou
>   Thron'd in easy state to reign;
> Thou art God, whose arms of love
>   Aching, spent, the world sustain.

W. H. Vanstone

'Mother, there is your son' . . . 'There is your mother.'

John 19.26–7

The camera of the passion story now turns to a very different scene. It fastens, not on a brigand in his death-throes, but on a holy, lovely woman in middle life and on her son. The bond between them must have been very close, and their love for one another very deep. They had shared exile when Herod sought to kill the little boy. She had been there, more than likely, when the townspeople in Nazareth had tried to throw him over the cliff, after his first sermon in their synagogue (Luke 4.28–30). She had shared his sense of rejection when the popularity in which he was held turned to opposition and then to rank hatred. She who had shared his dangers now shared his final suffering, making his agony her own. A sword was piercing to her heart, as the aged Simeon had foretold (Luke 2.35). His 'hour' was hers too.

The tragedy numbed her – the tragedy of a life cut short. Only thirty-three! Why, Alexander had died about that age, but *he* had conquered the world! The life of her son had been so full of promise. He had grown in wisdom (mentally) and stature (physically), in favour with God (spiritually) and with men and women (socially) – Luke spelt it out so carefully (2.40 and 52). He could have had the world at his feet. And now, she could only avert her eyes.

Nonetheless, the relation between mother and son had not always been easy. There had been that occasion when the parents had had to rebuke the boy for staying in Jerusalem while they and their party had set out on the return journey to the north: 'My son, why have you treated us like this?' (Luke 2.48). And *he* had had to rebuke *her* when, at the wedding feast, she had drawn his attention to the lack of wine. He had had to reply: 'That is no concern of mine. My hour has not yet come' (John 2.4). It cannot have been easy for Mary to be kept waiting outside the house while he was teaching the crowd inside and then for her to receive the message: 'Here are my mother and my brothers. Whoever does the will of God is my brother and sister and *mother*' (Mark 3.31–5). If Jesus felt the tension between the absolute demands of the heavenly Father and the demands of his parents, we may be sure that Mary experienced that tension too.

But, now, all that is passed and the end has nearly come. He is on the cross and she is at its foot. Soon she will be bereft, alone with her grief, her loss, and her memories. No longer will she be able to look after his needs, the washing and the mending of his clothes, the provision of food for his journeys, all the little comforts she had loved to provide for him. What will she do without him in the long years that stretch ahead?

Then there was John. Young, deeply sensitive, spiritually perceptive, his was the kind of nature which felt life's tragedies and bereavements more excruciatingly than does the ordinary run of humankind. Others of the Twelve might be able to get on without the physical presence of their master – but John? The relationship between the man of thirty-three and the younger man, possibly hardly out of his teens, had been peculiarly close. Now it was about to be broken. The parting was near. What would John do?

Two people in deep need. Jesus looked down at them both, and his heart went out to them in a deep, self-forgetting compassion. Different from one another though Mary and John were, their primary needs were the same. Each would need companionship. Each would need work to do. The diagnosis was sure; the remedy lay in themselves.

Companionship. Mary needed another 'son' to love and to care for. John needed another 'mother' to protect and to guard and, if it might be, to guide into new paths of usefulness. So from the cross came the words of mutual commendation: 'Mother, there is your son' . . . 'There is your mother.' 'And from that moment', the evangelist tells us, 'the disciple took her into his home' (John 19.27).

I find this a deeply moving story. I find it also an intensely practical one. Bereavement is about the most painful thing that can come the way of any of us, and it is so easy, so understandably easy, for the bereaved to slip into a slough of despond and of self-pity. This story of Jesus and his ministry to Mary and John points in the direction of a healing answer. 'Find someone in need', it says to us, 'and look after him or her. Even if the heavens are so clouded that looking *up*, you cannot see any signs of sunshine, look *around* you and discover some other person in need or distress or loneliness, and start to

25

minister to him or her. That may prove to be the beginning of healing for you.'

This is not to run away from sorrow. This is to sublimate it. The dictionary defines 'sublimate' as 'to act upon (a substance) so as to produce a refined product'. God may graciously 'act upon' you and 'produce a refined' character, after his own pattern. Then it may not be overlong before you find a rift in the clouds, no bigger than a man's hand at the start but steadily getting bigger. Once again you will see the sunshine of God's face.

In the last chapter of Paul's letter to the Romans, there is a list of people to whom he sends his greetings. We do not generally linger long over these verses; a catalogue of persons unknown to us is not enthralling, and most of those mentioned were people of no great eminence, just ordinary people whom the apostle had met on his travels and whom he had influenced and whose friendship he had enjoyed. But the name of one of them was Rufus (?red-head), and I pause when I come to his name in the list. Paul sends greetings to him 'and to his mother, *whom I call mother too*' (Romans 16.13). It is a nice touch. On his travels, when the voyage had been rough and the reception even rougher, Paul needed a woman to look after him in the ports where he disembarked. Rufus' mother had met that need, and he was less lonely because of her care. Mary and John, John and Mary, Paul and Rufus' mother . . . .

There are many who need just that sort of care today in our sophisticated society. Great conurbations, for all their teeming millions, can be lonely places. So can universities, as many an undergraduate, away from home for the first time, finds to their cost. Bedsitters can be lonely places, too. Black people can be lonely when they live in a predominantly white environment, and so can people of faiths other than ours who are puzzled by our English reserve and by our paganism. And transients .... So we could go on. An open front door, a shared meal, a welcome to the family fireside. 'Mother, there is your son.' 'There is your mother.'

Inasmuch as we do it to the least of one of his brethren, we do it to the Lord Christ himself. A ministry awaits us, such as that which awaited Mary and John and Rufus' mother.

Lord, as we stand at the cross with Mary
and hear your words,
still caring even in your agony,
we ask you to work in us your desire;
that as humble members of your family
we may care deeply for each other,
and unselfishly commend your love
in word and deed.

Roger Pickering

Dear Lord, who hast blessed us with the gift of family
life, that we may learn to love and care for others: we
praise thee for the example of thy Son Jesus Christ, who
even when deserted and betrayed by closest friends took
thought for his mother and his disciple. Open our eyes
to recognise in all people the claims of kinship, and stir
our hearts to serve them as our brothers and sisters called
with us into the family of thy love.

Basil Naylor

O Lord Jesus Christ,
    fill me with that love of thine
    wherewith out of thine own pain
        thou didst comfort thy Mother in hers;
    and despoiled and naked
        gavest her both home and son.
To such love, without like, without limit,
    lead me, O Lord,
        now and for ever.

Eric Milner-White

4

The Agony of Doubt

From midday a darkness fell over the whole land, which lasted until three in the afternoon; and about three Jesus cried aloud, 'Eli, Eli, lama sabachthani?' which means, 'My God, my God, why have you forsaken me?' Hearing this, some of the bystanders said, 'He is calling Elijah.' One of them ran at once and fetched a sponge, which he soaked in sour wine and held to his lips at the end of a stick. But the others said, 'Let us see if Elijah will come to save him.'

Jesus again cried aloud and breathed his last.

Matthew 27.45–50

Spent didst thou fall that thou mightest my soul gain;
To save me thou didst bear the cross's pain;
May not so great a labour be in vain.

*W. H. Vanstone's translation of the
lines from* Dies Irae

'My God, my God, why have you forsaken me?'

*O*f all the seven words from the cross, this, surely, is the most mysterious. Here, more than in any of the others, it is hard to penetrate. We might as well admit that we shall never fully fathom the meaning of this word.

If sin appals *us*, how much more must it have appalled *him* who was totally pure! And the cross is the place where heaven's purity and earth's sin meet. When that happens, there is mystery, darkness, smoke. When the holiness of the Lord, 'high and exalted', and the sinfulness of Isaiah, 'a man of unclean lips', met, 'the house began to fill with smoke' (Isaiah 6.1–7). Jesus was carrying a load the like of which none of us will ever be called upon to bear. 'He carried our sins in his own person on the gibbet', that was how Peter put it in his first Letter (1 Peter 2.24). It was a crushing load which blotted out for Jesus the consciousness of the presence of the God who had meant more to him, all his life, than anyone or anything else. A sense of sheer, stark dereliction swept over him. If the cross is the place where God's disgust with sin and his burning love for humankind meet in terrible expression; if God in Christ is there clearing up the mess made by a rebel race, can we wonder that there is mystery? We can dare to look – and adore.

> O generous love! that he, who smote
> In Man for man the foe,
> The double agony in Man
> For man should undergo.

33

There is one facet of this 'agony', as reflected in the fourth word, on which I want to fasten here. As I listened to it, I found myself giving 'The Agony of Doubt' as the title of this meditation. Granted that doubt is only part of the mystery here, had I any right to use this word in connection with the man who hung and suffered there? Is it not sinful to doubt? Jesus, so we hold, was sinless. Where is this word, where is this comment leading us?

There are various kinds of doubt. I believe there is a kind of doubt which is sinful. It springs from the attitude of people who do not seriously want to find a living faith in God. Rather, they welcome an excuse behind which they can shelter from the onslaught of truth and its challenge to mind and conscience. They are not prepared to face the facts and assess the evidence. They reject some puerile presentation of the faith given them when they were young, reject it as if it were the real thing. They refuse to give time and care to the consideration of a more adequate presentation of Christian truth which they as adults could appreciate. Rejecting the spurious as if it were the real, they become doubters, agnostics, perhaps atheists. Such doubt, surely, partakes of the nature of sin.

But there is another kind of doubt which is quite different and has little or nothing of sin about it. It springs from a person who is eagerly seeking for the truth. It is the questioning of an honest and enquiring mind. It can sometimes be the agony of a broken spirit which dares, even in the darkness, still to say 'My God', and yet must needs add 'Why?' and, at its darkest moment, 'Why have you forsaken me?' I repeat, there is

34

nothing sinful about that. To cry out like that is simply to admit our humanity with its necessary limitation of sight and understanding and its longing to penetrate the darkness. We cling on, if only by our finger-nails. We pray, if only the prayer of the distressed father who sought healing for his son: 'I believe; help my unbelief' (Mark 9.24).

To conceal this questioning, to repress it, or to attempt to swallow it – there is nothing very Christian about that. Indeed, such a reaction to doubt can be dangerous. It can lead to a revulsion from belief, and to a deeper darkness. Far better to have the questioning out with God, even to protest as psalmists and prophets did with astonishing boldness: 'Why stand far off, Lord? Why hide away in times of trouble?' (Psalm 10.1). 'How long, Lord, will you be deaf to my plea? "Violence!" I cry out to you, but you do not come to the rescue' (Habakkuk 1.2). Examples could be multiplied.

This cry from the cross compels us to face the question: how seriously do we take the doctrine of the humanity of Jesus? Maybe we acknowledge his divinity; we may even subscribe to the credal statement 'God from God, Light from Light, true God from true God'. But when it comes to the reality of his human nature, it is easy to slip into thinking in terms of a kind of phantom manhood. The New Testament protests. Listen to this from the writer of Hebrews – the passage casts a piercing light on the earthly experiences of Jesus and especially on the Gethsemane scene:

In the course of his earthly life he offered up prayers and petitions, with loud cries and tears, to God who was able to deliver him from death. Because of his devotion his prayer was heard: son though he was, *he learned obedience through his sufferings*. (Hebrews 5.7–8)

The Greeks had wrestled with the relation between suffering and learning. They had even made a pun out of their pondering: *pathos mathos*, suffering is learning. Jesus 'incarnated' the problem, worked it out in his own flesh and blood. I believe that, in his case, the suffering included the doubting, and perhaps the doubting was the sharpest part of the suffering. I take courage here. I see that now he *knows* because then he *knew*.

> In every pang that rends the heart
> The Man of sorrows had a part.

There are two minor points about this word that should be noted. *First*, the cry is a quotation, from the opening words of Psalm 22. From his boyhood days, Jesus had learnt the Scriptures, had been brought up on them, had fed his soul on them. When, before the beginning of his ministry, temptation assailed him in the wilderness, he rebutted the tempter with quotations from the book of Deuteronomy. Now, at the end of his ministry, when doubt and darkness assailed him with a force he had never known before, his mind reverted to Scripture, and in that Scripture he found words which seemed to express his need.

Second, it is worth noting that Psalm 22, though it begins in the depths of doubt and despair, ends with an expression of joyful confidence and hope: 'I shall declare your fame to my associates, praising you in the midst of the assembly. You that fear the Lord, praise him, hold him in honour . . . revere him . . . For he has not scorned him who is downtrodden but he has listened to his cry for help' (vv.22ff.). The psalmist has come out of the darkest cloud into the sunshine of God's face. So it was to be with our Lord. The cry 'My God, my God, why have you forsaken me?' is to be followed, almost at the last, by the victory cry 'Finished!' and, at the very end, with the peaceful commendation 'Father, into your hands I commit my spirit.'

To every sensitive person come moments when a sense of dereliction threatens to overwhelm them. What is the meaning of human history? Why the immensity of human suffering? Is Christianity a piece of make-believe? The death of a dear one, the sickness of another – is there not one clear word from beyond? Belief is easy when spring is in the air and everyone smiles on you. There are winter moments when all is dark. 'My God, my God, why . . .?'

Be of good courage, you who now are in darkness, whether it be the darkness of doubt or of bereavement or of any other kind. The sun is still there, though the clouds now are hiding it. The Father is still there, though his face seems to be hidden. Christ knows and understands, because he has been through experiences far worse than those you are now enduring. The darkness is not for ever.

Did you ever watch on television or in a garden an expert pruning a vine? I did. It seemed so cruel. But I noticed that the gardener was never nearer the vine than when he was pruning it.

I believe, help my unbelief.

Mark 9.24

The night is dark, and I am far from home –
Lead thou me on!

John Henry Newman

Our God, whose love never fails us, and from whom nothing but our self-will can finally separate us: We confess with shame the darkness of our sin that cast so deep a shadow on the cross; we thank thee for the glory of thy Son's obedience that carried him through the loneliness of his passion; and we pray that in the hour of our trial, when all is dark and there is no vision, we may be strengthened in our obedience and faith, knowing that the spirit of him who suffered alone will never leave us to endure alone.

Basil Naylor

O God, whose blessed Son endured the loneliness and darkness of the cross, that we might enjoy eternal fellowship with thee: Grant that amidst life's shadows we may know that we are never forsaken, but that we are ever walking in the light of thy countenance; through the same Jesus Christ our Lord.

Frank Colquhoun

5

A Passion for Obedience

After this, Jesus, aware that all had now come to its appointed end, said in fulfilment of scripture, 'I am thirsty.'

John 19.28

Late have I loved you, beauty so old and so new: late have I loved you . . . You were fragrant, and I drew in my breath and now pant after you. I tasted you, and I feel but hunger and thirst for you. You touched me, and I am set on fire to attain the peace which is yours.

St Augustine, Confessions

In his will is our peace.

Dante, The Divine Comedy

*W*e should take these words at their face value, to mean exactly what they say. The midday sun over Jerusalem can be very hot, and now it was beating down mercilessly on the tortured body of Jesus. He longed for a drink to quench his intolerable craving. It is likely that none of us who read these words has ever been thirsty, in this sense of the word. We can only guess what that suffering is like. The fifth word from the cross means what it says – 'I am thirsty.'

The cry has often been interpreted as an expression of Christ's yearning for the souls of men and women. That, surely, is a legitimate extension of its meaning. Mark tells us that when Jesus 'saw a large crowd, his heart went out to them, because they were like sheep without a shepherd' (Mark 6.34). It was an almost physical longing to reach them, to woo them, to embrace them, and to win them home where they belonged.

> Souls of men, why will ye scatter
> Like a crowd of frightened sheep?

The folly and the tragedy of it appalled him. God had made provision for the eternal welfare of his children, and there they were turning their backs on it and spurning the provision of his love! This could never be a matter of indifference to him; everything hung on their response. The craving in the soul of Jesus was like someone's longing for a drink to ease a raging thirst.

Both of these interpretations of this cry, the literal and the metaphorical, are legitimate. But as I peer into the meaning of the words, I want to go deeper. I see them as an expression of Jesus' passion to *do the will of God* – to the limit, through life at its busiest, through suffering, through the sense of dereliction by God and man, through to death and beyond.

The mother of Jesus had a like passion. Perhaps he 'caught' it from her, learnt it from her even in his earliest boyhood years. 'I am the Lord's servant,' she had said at the moment of her deepest perplexity, 'may it be as you have said' (Luke 1.38). In effect she had said 'Your will be done. This is my passion, my thirst.' When Jesus came to teach his disciples how to pray, he incorporated her prayer in his: 'Your will be done, on earth as in heaven.' Her passion was his.

The offering of the body of Jesus on the cross, unique as it was in its nature and its efficacy, was not an isolated act. Rather, it was the climax of a life-series of such acts of offering, their consummation. The whole purpose of his coming and of his mission was the doing of the will of God. 'Here I am . . .; I have come, O God, to do your will' (Hebrews 10.7). Just because, every day of his life, as it was increasingly revealed to him, he had made this his central intention, he could sum it all up in the final great offering of his body once for all on the cross. Had he not lived such a life, he could not have made such an offering or died such a death. This is the meaning of St Bernard's sentence: 'It was not the death of Jesus which pleased [God] but the willingness to die.' That was his supreme offering.

Maximilian Kolbe was a Polish priest. A brilliant student but with very frail health, he poured himself into his work in parish and in printing, founded a friary, went to Japan. Then came the holocaust. He and his friars were arrested and driven away. 'Take courage, my sons,' Kolbe said, 'we're setting off on a new mission – and we're having our fares paid for us. What a stroke of luck!' They came for him on 17 February, 1941, and took him to the prison in the centre of Warsaw and thence to Auschwitz concentration camp. In August, three prisoners escaped. For every man who escaped it was decreed that ten of his fellows must die. Two Nazis passed down the lines of prisoners, selecting their victims. One man cried out: 'My wife, my children, I shall never see them again.' Kolbe stepped out of the line, saluted, and offered himself in place of the man. By some extraordinary miracle, the offer was accepted, the man was reprieved, Kolbe died. This act of supreme heroism was not an isolated event. It was the last and greatest of a lifelong series of acts of obedience. As he had lived, so he died.

I find this word from the cross immensely stimulating and challenging. Though it was a word spoken almost at the moment of dying, I find in it a clue to living. It is the ideal prayer for early morning use. I am facing a new day, heavy with demand, big with opportunity. I look to God and say: 'I have come to do your will, O my God. I thirst to do it.' Or I am facing the challenge of a new job. I offer it to God for him to make of it what he will, through me. I say to him: 'I have come to this new job to do your will in it. I thirst to do it.' Or again, I am going on some errand at home or abroad, there are new problems to tackle, new people to meet. I say to God: 'I have come on this errand to do your will. I thirst to do it.' In this way, all life becomes an offering. Then, when death comes, that shall be an offering too, for it will be the entrance to a new life of worship and service, of unimaginable dimensions and of untold glory.

It is indeed strange that we should be frightened to live life along these lines. Many are frightened of the will of God – as if the Father's will could be anything other than the best for the welfare of his children! Some misguided hymn writers have written about the will of God as if it were something to be borne, endured, put up with, rather than to be welcomed with eager hands, embraced, and grappled to our souls with hoops of steel. What strange creatures we are! 'In his will is our peace' – there, and nowhere else.

People break down, crushed under life's load, because they will not believe this and act accordingly. It is a vast pity. Jesus said that the really happy people are actually those who 'hunger and thirst after righteousness. They will be satisfied' (Matthew 5.6). This contrasts sharply with those whose lives are spent in the fevered thirst after pleasure. It is an unrewarding business. It ends, not in satisfaction or peace but in a kind of hollow fatuity. Look at the faces of those who have spent their lives in this way and you will see living illustrations of the fact that, *out of* the will of God, there is no peace.

When the time comes to render our account to God, our offering will be a poor one when compared with Christ's perfect oblation. All too often the thirst, the longing to do God's will has been very far short of a passion; other things have intervened and we have sought to slake our thirst in brackish waters. But at least, day by day, we can keep this goal steadily before us — thirsting to do God's will, thirsting so to touch our fellow men and women that they may come to the knowledge of God in Christ, so that the final offering may have a wholeness about it, all its parts fused by the passion to know and to fulfil what God has in mind for the children of his love.

Almighty God, in whom we live and move and have our being, who hast made us for thyself, so that our hearts are restless till they rest in thee: Grant us purity of heart and strength of purpose, that no selfish passion may hinder us from knowing thy will, no weakness from doing it; but that in thy light we may see light clearly, and in thy service find thy perfect freedom; through Jesus Christ our Lord.

St Augustine

Son of Man, who endured in your body
    the agony of thirst in death,
and in your spirit thirsted
    for the world's salvation;
deepen our understanding of your sufferings
    by which our redemption was secured,
and increase in us those spiritual longings
    which you alone can satisfy;
that hungering and thirsting after righteousness
    we may be filled with all the fullness of God
and serve and praise you evermore.

Frank Colquhoun

O Lord Jesus Christ,
  Fill me with that thirst of thine
  for the will of God and for human souls
    proclaimed in the word 'I thirst':
That I may fear no bodily pains,
      if only thou givest me the cup of obedience
          and love
      to drink with thee,
        when thou wilt and as thou wilt;
          for thine endless mercies' sake.

Eric Milner-White

6

The Triumph of Faithfulness

Having received the wine, he said, 'It is accomplished!' Then he bowed his head and gave up his spirit.

John 19.30

I have glorified you on earth by finishing the work which you gave me to do.

John 17.4

'It is accomplished!'

John 19.30

*I*t well might not have been. Suppose that Jesus had yielded to the tempter's suggestion that what the people wanted was food for the belly, while Jesus knew that what they needed was God's word. Suppose that he had yielded to the tempter's suggestion that what the people wanted was fun and excitement, while Jesus knew that what they needed was life with the quality of eternity. Suppose he had yielded to the tempter's suggestion that what the people wanted was force, powerful leadership which would drive the Romans into the sea, while Jesus knew that what they needed was the worship of God worked out in service to their fellows (Matthew 4.1–11). Suppose that Jesus had heeded Peter's enticing word when, the shadow of the cross looming large over his master's path, he had remonstrated with him: 'Heaven forbid! No, Lord, this shall never happen to you.' Suppose that at that crucial moment there had been no horrified rebuttal: 'Out of my sight, Satan, you are a stumbling-block to me. You think as men think, not as God thinks' (Matthew 16.21–3). Suppose that in the garden of Gethsemane Jesus had inverted the prayer and said 'Not your will but mine be done.' Suppose that as the call of God came constantly to him during his life, he had settled for less than the best.

Suppose! What then? At the last, as he looked up into the Father's face, Jesus could not have cried 'Accomplished! Completed!' He would have had an *in*complete offering to make to God. Our liturgy could

53

never have contained, as contain it does in the version of 1662, the words 'a full, perfect, and sufficient sacrifice, oblation, and satisfaction, for the sins of the whole world'.

The temptation of Jesus was long drawn out. Not without meaning does Luke end his story of the wilderness temptation with the words 'the devil departed, biding his time' (4.13). There is something sinister in the suggestion that the devil was not content with his defeat – he would be back again! And so, no doubt, it was; temptation assailed Jesus from the opening consciousness of his boyhood, through adolescence and young manhood, through the years of busy ministry, up to the cross and during its final agony. There was no let-up. But always the response was negative to the tempter, positive to the Father. So, as the physical life of Jesus came near to its closing, his penultimate cry was one not of defeat but of triumph, as his ultimate cry was to be one of total peace: 'Father, into your hands . . .'.

In this cry 'It is accomplished' – the Latin *consummatum est* says it well – we see the first ray of Easter light. We cannot, and must not, separate Good Friday and Easter Day. Christian theology and Christian experience have always held them together, inseparably. Good Friday (which is, of course, a corruption of God's Friday) would have been the devil's field-day if it had not been for the event of Easter. It would have signalled the final triumph of evil, the ultimate victory of all that was demonic gathering together its forces against all that was holy and lovely and just and true – and winning the day. It would have been to assert that at the heart of the universe is not love but nonsense, and that all we can say about life is that

54

'it is a tale, told by an idiot, full of sound and fury, signifying nothing'.

The older translations of this sixth word from the cross say 'It is finished.' But we cannot leave it at that. Everything depends on how you utter the word 'finished', and in what tone. If the tone is minor, 'finished' could indicate defeat and hint that the speaker is himself 'finished', done in, defeated in the battle. But the meaning of the original forbids such an interpretation. The tone is a major one. The tense is a perfect one: 'it has been and will for ever remain finished'. 'We note the achievement Jesus claimed just before he died. It is not men who have finished their brutal deed; it is he who has accomplished what he came into the world to do' (John Stott). The word is the shout of a king, albeit a king on a cross. It is the declaration of a victory achieved: 'I have glorified you on earth by finishing the work which you gave me to do' (John 17.4).

James Stewart, that fine New Testament scholar and preacher, wrote of that cry when death and darkness were irrevocably defeated:

> Our Christian faith is that at that moment of victory the whole human prospect was changed. At that point in history there was a new creation, the daybreak of the world. And the ratification was the resurrection. In one irreducibly miraculous act, baffling all human explanation, God raised him on high, and gave him a name above every name. And the early Church took up the shout. 'Christ reigns,' shouted the martyrs at the stake;

and went down into the darkness shouting it; and passed shouting to the throne of God.

It is small cause for surprise that, at my enthronement at Canterbury, I took as the text for my sermon the words in John's Gospel: 'In the world you shall have tribulation. But be of good cheer, I have overcome the world' (16.33). I said:

It is time that we said, unitedly and joyfully, to all who will listen: 'We are not interested in the possibility of defeat. Our confidence is in the risen Lord, who said "On this rock I will build my Church and the gates of hell shall not prevail against it." We know something of the power of the Holy Spirit. We are open to learn more of him. We await the surprises of tomorrow.'

'It is accomplished' is a cry, a rallying cry, which the Church needs to hear and to heed today. If that cry is heeded, it spells an end to that almost morbid self-denigration and defeatism which has marked some sections of the Church for all too long. We follow a crucified Christ. We would follow no other. But we follow a Christ who, at the moment when men thought they had defeated him, saw that he had defeated the forces of evil and cried: 'Accomplished! Consummated! Achieved!' Here is our hope.

We who are baptised into Christ, who have taken up our cross to follow him, are heirs of that hope. True, the forces of evil are on the rampage and we are in the midst of the conflict. But their final defeat is guaranteed, for, as we affirm at every Eucharist, 'Christ has died: Christ is risen: Christ will come again.'

So, while our heads are bent over the world's pain and sickness and sin, and our backs ache in doing our part in alleviating them, our hearts are sustained by the triumph of faith. 'It is accomplished!'

Lift up your hearts.

We lift them to the Lord.

O Lord God, Lamb of God, Son of the Father, that takest away the sins of the world: Grant that as thy sacrifice for our redemption was full, perfect, and sufficient, so nothing may be wanting in our service and sacrifice for thee as members of thy mystical body; for the honour and glory of thy holy name.

Frank Colquhoun

O Lord Christ, as we thankfully recall thy finished work for the redemption of the world, so we pray that we may ever be mindful of the unfinished task which thou hast committed to thy Church; that constrained by thy love we may labour to share thy saving gospel with all human-kind, for the furtherance of thy kingdom and the glory of thy name.

Frank Colquhoun

O Lord Jesus Christ,
    Endue me with that strength of thine
    wherewith thou didst resolve upon the Father's
             work,
        and utterly accomplish it:
That in the morning and evening I may do
          his will;
  and when night cometh and no one can work,
      I may say with thee and unto thee,
          "It is finished":
      to the glory of thy holy Name.

Eric Milner-White

O Lord God, when thou givest to thy servants to endeavour any great matter,
grant us also to know that it is not the beginning, but the
continuing of the same, until it be thoroughly finished,
which yieldeth the true glory;
through him who for the finishing of thy work laid down
his life for us, our Redeemer, Jesus Christ.

After Sir Francis Drake

7

The Peace of Surrender

By now it was about midday and a darkness fell over the whole land, which lasted until three in the afternoon: the sun's light failed. And the curtain of the temple was torn in two. Then Jesus uttered a loud cry and said, 'Father, into your hands I commit my spirit'; and with these words he died. When the centurion saw what had happened, he gave praise to God. 'Beyond all doubt,' he said, 'this man was innocent.'

Luke 23.44–7

Surely for the Christian, death is the greatest healing of all.

Russ Parker

'Father, into your hands I commit my spirit'

Luke 23.46

I t might be thought that 'surrender' is a strange word to use in a title for this last word from the cross. Of course, there are various kinds of surrender. There is, for example, the surrender which takes place at the end of some terrible war when the leaders of the defeated forces, hard-faced and bitter, in the presence of the victorious generals sign terms of surrender – terms which in themselves may well contain the seeds of yet another conflagration. That is one kind of surrender.

But there is another kind. Here are two young people; or perhaps not so young. They have come to know one another, their interests and common concerns, their family backgrounds, their circles of friends, and they decide to 'go it together' in marriage. Such a decision is consummated in total surrender, the one to the other, in a life-long commitment of love, 'for better for worse, for richer for poorer, in sickness and in health, till death us do part'. There is no bitterness of surrender here. There is costliness, of course; there is seriousness of intent. But this surrender of love brings with it an integration of personality, a harmony of minds, a peace rarely known outside the marriage bond. This kind of surrender has no bitterness about it. It is the surrender of peace.

This last word from the cross partakes of the nature of this second kind of surrender, not of the first. There is no kind of bitterness here, no cry of a man defeated in battle. This, on the contrary, is the surrender of love, not indeed in a marriage relationship but in the relationship of the total understanding of a son with his father.

Like the fourth word from the cross ('My God, my God, why have you forsaken me?'), this seventh word is a quotation from the Psalms (31.5). The Scriptures which had proved to be Christ's stay and strength during his life are now proving to be just that in the hours of his dying. But this is more than a quotation from Psalm 31, for Jesus does what the psalmist does not: he prefaces the words 'into your hands I commit my spirit' with the vocative 'Father'.

The New Testament scholar Joachim Jeremias has taught us that the use of the word *Abba* (Father) is a singularly intimate way of expressing a father–son relationship. It is difficult to find an English equivalent. 'Daddy' would be too familiar and too juvenile, though not too intimate. Clearly it will not do. Perhaps 'dear father' is the best we can suggest. *Abba* is the word that Jesus used and encouraged his disciples to join him in using. So, as the liturgy has it, 'we are bold to say 'Our Father'.' As his life draws to its close, Jesus no longer cries 'my God', but resumes the designation which he seems most commonly to have used: 'Father, dear Father'.

'The hands of God' – a striking phrase! To speak of God in this way is to engage in what the theologians call anthropomorphic language, that is to say, to speak of God as if he were human. God is spirit; he has no hands. But, because we are human and our minds are limited by human concepts, we must needs speak of God in human terms – his eyes, his fingers, his hands. When we speak of the hands of God we know what we mean, for hands are those parts of our anatomy which, above all other parts, get things done. So, when the psalmist says 'Your hands made me and formed me' (Psalm 119.73), he is thinking of the *creative* activity of God. Here, in the verse from Psalm 31, from which Jesus quotes the first part 'into your hands I commit my spirit', he seems to be thinking of the *redemptive* activity of God, for he goes on, 'You have delivered me (redeemed me), Lord, you God of truth.' It is, then, to a mighty creator and a loving redeemer that Jesus commits himself at the end of his earthly journey. That being so, there can be nothing to fear. The hands that made him and formed him are there to receive him. All is well.

If this is the ultimate truth for the Christian, why should we fear death? Why not welcome it as a friend, as did Francis of Assisi in his *Canticle of the Sun*:

> And thou most kind and gentle death,
> Waiting to hush our latest breath,
>   O praise him! Alleluia!
> Thou leadest home the child of God,
> And Christ our Lord the way hath trod,
>   Alleluia!

It is true that the accompaniments of death – the weakness, the helplessness, the dependency on others – are often humiliating. It is true that there is the sharpness of separation from loved ones and the natural grief that goes with it, and there is nothing to be ashamed of in that. But death itself – why soft-pedal it? Why skirt around it? Why muffle up reference to it? If in fact it is surrender, commitment into the hands of him who mightily created us and mercifully redeemed us, should there not be a quiet confidence about our anticipation of death and even a note of gladness as we approach it?

Grow old along with me!
The best is yet to be,
The last of life, for which the first was made:
Our times are in His hand
Who saith, 'A whole I planned,
Youth shows but half; trust God: see all, nor be afraid!'

Those are fine words of Robert Browning. 'The best is yet to be' is pertinent to *all* stages of a Christian's life. If she is *young*, life stretches ahead, full of opportunities to serve Christ in a world in dire need of such service as she can offer. There is only one master worthy of total dedication, and that is the Lord Christ.

If the Christian is in *middle-life*, with all the responsibilities which those years bring to most of us, then she can say – and mean – 'the best is yet to be'. For in the companionship of Christ and in the strength of his Spirit, she can face the future with that serenity which belongs to the heirs of his legacy: 'Peace is my parting gift to you, my own peace, such as the world cannot give. Set your troubled hearts at rest, and banish your fears' (John 14.27).

If the Christan is *old*, she can still say – and mean – 'the best is yet to be'. Browning had in mind the latter part of our physical life, 'the last of life for which the first was made'. And he was right; within those limits, there should be depth of living, a maturity of relationships which is richer in old age than, in the nature of the case, it can be in youth or even in the hurried middle years.

For the Christian disciple, these words of Browning have a wider reference than that which was immediately in the mind of the poet. 'The best is yet to be' – beyond the river of death. 'Yea, though I walk through the valley of the shadow of death, I will fear no evil: for thou art with me . . . (Psalm 23.4) – the Prayer Book translation is specific in its reference to death. The *Revised English Bible* is probably more accurate and is wider in its inclusiveness: 'Even were I to walk through a valley of deepest darkness I should fear no harm, for you are with me.' If an Old Testament writer could be conscious of a presence with him in the darkest valley – be it of life or of death – how much more conscious, and confident, should the Christian be!

David Watson, that charismatic Anglican leader, fought a long battle with cancer. As he faced death, he wrote to his friends and quoted Browning: 'The best is yet to be.' Indeed that is the title of the last chapter of his biography by Teddy Saunders and Hugh Sansom. For him, Christ had 'broken the power of death and brought life and immortality to light through the gospel' (2 Timothy 1.10). There was a light on the other side! Like Mr Standfast in Bunyan's *Pilgrim's Progress*, as he came to the river, he could say with confidence: 'Now methinks I stand easie.' The old promise, 'when you pass through water I shall be with you; when you pass through rivers they will not overwhelm you' (Isaiah 43.2), held firm.

Richard Baxter, seventeenth-century Puritan divine and prolific author, echoes this approach to death and writes with a kind of glad carefreeness:

> Lord, it belongs not to my care
> Whether I die or live;
> To love and serve thee is my share,
> And this thy grace must give.
>
> Christ leads us through no darker rooms
> Than he went through before:
> And he that to God's Kingdom comes
> Must enter by this door.
>
> My knowledge of that life is small,
> The eye of faith is dim;
> But 'tis enough that Christ knows all,
> And I shall be with him.

In another hymn, he pursues his theme further, confident that, on the other side of death, is reunion with those in Christ whom we have loved and lost awhile. He dares to write:

> As for my friends, they are not lost;
> The several vessels of thy fleet,
> Though parted now, by tempest tossed,
> Shall safely in the haven meet.

'The best is yet to be.'

'Father, into your hands I commit my spirit.'

Thanks be to God.

Abba, Father, in whom the Saviour trusted as in life so in death: We bless thee for this last prayer which marked the work accomplished, the end achieved; grant us so strong a faith and so ready an obedience that when our life on earth draws to its close, we may not fear to surrender it into thy hands as to an all-wise and all-loving Father; through the same Jesus Christ our Lord.

Basil Naylor

O heavenly Father, in whose hands are the hearts of all thy children: Grant us the faith that commits all to thee, without question and without reserve; that trusting ourselves wholly to thy love and wisdom, we may meet all that life may bring, and death itself at last, with serenity and courage; through thy Son Jesus Christ our Lord.

Frank Colquhoun

Father of mercies and God of love,
    in his last word from the cross
your Son our Saviour committed his spirit
    into your hands.
We today would do the same.
In your hands alone we are secure:
    there is no other place where we would be.
And so, our Father, receive us now,
as into your hands we commit ourselves,
    our souls and bodies,
in life and in death,
for time and for eternity.

Frank Colquhoun

Approach to the Cross

O Lord Christ, Lamb of God, Lord of Lords,
   call us, who are called to be saints,
     along the way of thy Cross:
draw us, who would draw nearer our King,
   to the foot of thy Cross:
cleanse us, who are not worthy to approach,
   with the pardon of thy Cross:
instruct us, the ignorant and blind,
   in the school of thy Cross:
arm us, for the battles of holiness,
   by the might of thy Cross:
bring us, in the fellowship of thy sufferings
   to the victory of thy Cross:
and seal us in the kingdom of thy glory
   among the servants of thy Cross,
   O crucified Lord;
who with the Father and the Holy Ghost
   livest and reignest one God
   almighty, eternal,
     world without end.

Eric Milner-White

Sources and Acknowledgements

At the end of each meditation I have added two or three relevant prayers, in order to help readers turn thinking into praying, if they so will. For these prayers I am particularly indebted to:

Canon Frank Colquhoun, *Parish Prayers* and
  Contemporary Parish Prayers
Eric Milner-White, *A Procession of Passion Prayers*
  and *My God, My Glory*.

The Bible text used is that of the *Revised English Bible* (Oxford and Cambridge University Presses 1989).

The publishers and I are grateful to the copyright holders for their permission to reproduce copyright material.

Chapter 1

Ralph Wright, 'Two Trees', from *Simpler Towards the Evening* (The Golden Quill Press 1983), p. 64.
Eric Milner-White, *A Procession of Passion Prayers* (SPCK 1950), p. 100.
George Timms (after C.J. Vaughan), *Parish Prayers* (Hodder & Stoughton 1967), no. 258.
Michael Botting, *Contemporary Parish Prayers* (Hodder & Stoughton 1975), no. 104.

Chapter 2

Edward Shillito, *Jesus of the Scars*.

J.S. Whale, *Christian Doctrine* (CUP 1941), pp. 186–7.

D.S. Brewer, *The Cambridge Review*, 27 February 1984.

Frank Colquhoun, *Contemporary Parish Prayers*, no. 105.

Basil Naylor, *Parish Prayers*, no. 260.

Eric Milner-White, *A Procession of Passion Prayers*,
    p. 102.

Chapter 3

W.H. Vanstone *Love's Endeavour, Love's Expense* (DLT
    1977), pp. 119–20.

Roger Pickering, *Contemporary Parish Prayers*, no. 109.

Basil Naylor, *Parish Prayers,* no. 265.

Eric Milner-White, *A Procession of Passion Prayers*,
    p. 104.

Chapter 4

W.H. Vanstone, *Love's Endeavour, Love's Expense*, p. 57.

J.H. Newman, 'Praise to the Holiest in the Height',
    from 'The Dream of Gerontius', *Verses on Various
    Occasions*, (1874) pp. 265–6.

J.H. Newman, from 'Lead, Kindly Light', from *Verses
    on Various Occasions*, p. 114.

Basil Naylor, *Parish Prayers,* no. 269.

Frank Colquhoun, *Parish Prayers*, no. 272.

Chapter 5

St. Augustine, *Confessions* X. xxvii (38). Translated by
    Henry Chadwick (OUP 1991), p. 201.

Dante, *The Divine Comedy, Paradiso*, iii 85.

St. Augustine, *Parish Prayers*, no. 1602.

Chapter 6

John Stott, *The Cross of Christ* (IVP 1986), p. 82.

James Stewart, *King for Ever* (Abingdon 1975), p. 14.

Frank Colquhoun, *Parish Prayers*, no. 280.

Frank Colquhoun, *Parish Prayers*, no. 281.

Eric Milner-White, *A Procession of Passion Prayers*, p. 110.

After Sir Francis Drake, *Parish Prayers*, no. 1614.

Chapter 7

Russ Parker, *Free to Fail* (Triangle/SPCK 1992), p. 46.

St Francis of Assisi (1182–1226), *Canticle of the Sun*.

Robert Browning (1812–1889), from 'Rabbi ben Ezra' from *Dramatis Personae* (1864).

Teddy Saunders and Hugh Sansom, *David Watson: A Biography* (Hodder & Stoughton 1992).

Richard Baxter (1615–1691), from 'Lord, it belongs not to my care', verses 1, 3, and 6, and 'He wants not friends that hath thy love', verse 3.

Basil Naylor, *Parish Prayers*, no. 282.

Frank Colquhoun, *Parish Prayers*, no. 285.

Frank Colquhoun, *Contemporary Parish Prayers*, no. 121.

Eric Milner-White, *My God, My Glory* (SPCK 1954), p. 48.

Also published by

TRI∆NGLE

PRAYERS FOR TODAY
by Frank Colquhoun

A short book of prayers which deal with matters of
common experience, grouped around the Life of the
Everyday, the Christian Pilgrimage and the World We
Live In.

PRAYERS FOR EVERYONE
by Frank Colquhoun

A wide-ranging collection of prayers with something
for everyone, including prayers of Christian devotion,
and material from the Celtic tradition.

FAMILY PRAYERS
by Frank Colquhoun

Prayers and thanksgivings for all family occasions. It
looks at times of joy, sadness, change and celebration.

FREE TO FAIL
by Russ Parker

Looks at the place of failure in the Christian life. 'Russ Parker reveals a balance between pastoral sensitivity and biblical insight, which makes it such a compelling read.'   *Salvationist*

THE EDGE OF GLORY
Prayers in the Celtic Tradition
by David Adam

'It is a style that beautifully combines God's glory with everyday events. Containing prayers for individual devotions and corporate worship, they all express joyful faith in God.'   *Christian Family*

THE EYE OF THE EAGLE
Meditations on the Hymn 'Be thou my vision'
by David Adam

Explores the varied aspects of vision using a popular hymn to discover the spiritual riches which are hidden in the lives of us all.

GOD IN OUR MIDST
Prayers and devotions in the Celtic tradition
by Martin Reith

'A collection that vibrates with the Glory of the
Presence and that extends our vision of ourselves and
our world. To share in it is to lay ourselves open to
change and to glory.'   David Adam

ROUGH WAYS IN PRAYER
How can I pray when I feel spiritually dead?
by Paul Wallis
Foreword by Joyce Huggett

A lively and practical guide for times when personal
prayer seems hard.

The PRAYING WITH series,
books making accessible the words of some of the great
characters and traditions of faith for use by all
Christians:

PRAYING WITH SAINT AUGUSTINE
Introduction by Murray Watts

PRAYING WITH SAINT FRANCIS
Introduction by David Ford

PRAYING WITH THE NEW TESTAMENT
Introduction by Joyce Huggett

PRAYING WITH SAINT TERESA
Introduction by Elaine Storkey

PRAYING WITH THE JEWISH TRADITION
Introduction by Lionel Blue

PRAYING WITH HIGHLAND CHRISTIANS
Foreword by Sally Magnusson

PRAYING WITH THE OLD TESTAMENT
Introduction by Richard Holloway

PRAYING WITH THE ORTHODOX
TRADITION
Preface by Kallistos Ware

PRAYING WITH THE ENGLISH HYMN
WRITERS
Compiled and Introduced by Timothy Dudley-Smith

PRAYING WITH THE ENGLISH MYSTICS
Compiled and Introduced by Jenny Robertson

PRAYING WITH THE ENGLISH TRADITION
Preface by Robert Runcie

PRAYING WITH THE ENGLISH POETS
Compiled and Introduced by Ruth Etchells

PRAYING WITH THE MARTYRS
Preface by Madeleine L'Engle

PRAYING WITH JOHN DONNE AND GEORGE
HERBERT
Preface by Richard Harries

TRI∆NGLE
Books
can be obtained from
all good bookshops.
In case of difficulty,
or for a complete list of our books,
contact:
SPCK Mail Order
36 Steep Hill
Lincoln
LN2 1LU
(tel: 0522 527 486)